1.00

DEVOTIONS
and
PRAYERS
of
MARTIN LUTHER

D1453106

Selected and Translated
by
DR. ANDREW KOSTEN

BAKER BOOK HOUSE
Grand Rapids, Michigan

Copyright 1965 by
Baker Book House Company

ISBN: 0-8010-5582-2

Library of Congress
Catalog Card Number: 56-7581

Third printing, March 1983

Printed in the United States of America

FOREWORD

It has never been entirely forgotten that Martin Luther was a man of prayer and that he gave to the world many excellent models of public and private devotion. However, it seems to have been left to our generation, at least in so far as the English-speaking world is concerned, really to appreciate the richness and contemporaneity of the devotional treasures which are scattered throughout his voluminous writings.

Perhaps it is because our hearts are anxious today and, living as we are in a world which sometimes seems to be teetering on the brink of destruction, we are able to apprehend the depth of Luther's concern. Or perhaps it is because we have recovered such sympathy with the theology of the Reformation that we can understand afresh what the Word of God meant to him and what he meant by that divine grace which makes us acceptable to God even in our sin. Be this as it may, there is no doubt that the Reformer's prayers, sermons, and formal or informal comments on the Bible speak to us today across the chasm of the centuries and leave our hearts strangely warmed.

The compiler and translator of this little collection deserves our thanks for sharing with us something of what he has so obviously found helpful and precious in his own life.

Theodore G. Tappert

Preface

To know Martin Luther at his best, one must become acquainted with him as a man of devotion. No man sought the face of Christ more eagerly, prayed more fervently, or nourished his life by meditation more joyously than Luther. He was one of the greatest reformers, teachers and preachers of the Christian Church. His many-sided genius enabled him to excel in devotional literature as he excelled in almost everything else he turned to. His own devotional life is a classic example of Christianity: In meditating he saw the Heavens opened; his daily work was a prayer and prayer was his daily work. Even in the busiest periods of the Reformation Luther averaged two hours of prayer daily.

The format, size and arrangement of these fifty-two devotions are designed for the person with too little time to read a long book. Dwelling upon a single meditation and prayer each week, one will have several prayers committed to memory and a better understanding of about one-third of the Psalms at the end of a year. Nothing harms meditation more than the pressure of time. The busy man or woman can carry this volume in a pocket or purse. Leisurely reading of each devotion need take no more than five minutes.

Those meditations have been chosen for inclusion which provide answers to today's problems. All of them are spiritual gems — rich in comfort, counsel and inspiration.

Each prayer and meditation has been translated from the standard German texts of Luther's work.* I have used liberty as a translator in making Luther speak English. Some of this material has never before been translated into English. A few of the prayers may be familiar to Lutherans, but even there a fresh translation engenders new ideas. Old and familiar texts often fail to evoke the desired spiritual response, for the lips can say them without meshing with the mind that thinks them. I am indebted to Strodach's critical studies on Luther's prayers (Paul Z. Strodach, **Works of Martin Luther**, Vol. VI, Philadelphia, 1932); to Mr. Herman Baker and Mr. Cornelius Zylstra of Baker Book House for suggesting and designing this volume.

My hope is that the great Head of the

---

*Erlangen Edition: **Dr. M. Luthers Saemmtliche Werke.** 1828-1869, 67 Vols.

Walch Edition: **Martin Luthers Saemmtliche Schriften.** Herausgegeben von Johann Georg Walch, 1739-1753, 24 Vols.

Weimar Edition: **D. Martin Luthers, Kritische Gesamtausgabe,** Weimar: Herman Boehlaus Nachfolger, 1883 unfinished, 87 Vols. total.

Church may use these devotions to accomplish the purpose envisioned in Luther's own prayer: "Dear Lord, strengthen and increase thy faith in us. Amen."

Andrew W. Kosten

What Is Blessedness?

1

Blessed is the man that walketh not in the counsel of the ungodly, nor standeth in the way of sinners, nor sitteth in the seat of the scornful. But his delight is in the law of the Lord. — *Psalm 1:1, 2*

MEN are concerned with blessedness. There is no one who does not wish that it may be well with him, and does not dread the thought that it should be ill with him. Yet all have drifted from the knowledge of true blessedness. The philosophers have searched most diligently and erred most grievously, thinking blessedness to exist in virtue. They have only made themselves more unhappy than the rest by depriving themselves of the blessings both of this life and the life to come. The common people, on the other hand, have thought blessedness to consist of sensual pleasure. They have hoped, at least, to enjoy the good of this life.

The psalmist, drawing his doctrine from heaven and deploring all of man's efforts, gives this definition of blessedness: That man is blessed who loves the law of God. Blessed is the man who has found this pearl of great price. However, if he has not found this prize, he may search for the blessing of God without ever experiencing it.

Prayer

LORD God, heavenly Father, from whom we continuously receive all good things so lavishly, and by whom we are daily safe-guarded from all evil so graciously, help us, we beseech thee, to appropriate all these gifts through thy holy spirit with full heart and true faith, so that we may thank and praise thy gentle goodness and mercy; through Jesus Christ thy Son our Lord. Amen.

A Personal Application

2

I WILL emphasize, as many of the holy fathers have, that we should not wrongly sing or read the psalm as though it did not concern us. Rather we should use it to strengthen our faith and to comfort our consciences. The psalter is a school and exercise of our hearts and minds; so that he who reads it without understanding and faith reads it without the spirit.

When you read, for example, "Blessed is the man that walketh not in the counsel of the ungodly," you should take the words seriously, be terrified by the counsel of the ungodly, and pray with deep earnestness that you and other Christians may not be seduced by it. When you hear that the man is blessed whose desire is in the law of the Lord, you should not be dogmatic or boast that you love and desire the law, but ever cry to God, pleading from the heart that he will enkindle pleasure and love in you. Follow this method through the entire book.

Prayer

I AM certain that thou, God, art true and canst not lie. Enable me to be steadfast in faith, nothing doubting, not because of the merits of my prayer but because of the certainty of thy truth. Amen.

Comfort in Persecution

3

He that sitteth in the heavens shall laugh: the Lord shall have them in derision. — *Psalm 2:4.*

WHEN we are oppressed, how can we believe that God is holding our adversaries in derision! At such times it seems that we are reviled and derided by both God and man.

In the statement, "He that sitteth in the heavens shall laugh," the psalmist pictures the Lord as an invisible judge who is working to awaken and strengthen our hopes. He who cares for us is serene and fearless. Though we be disturbed, he remains unperturbed in caring for us. We are tossed to and fro, but he sits secure so that the righteous need not be forever uneasy.

This activity of God goes undetected, observable only if you were in heaven. But when suffering, as you through faith and hope rise above all, you receive him who sits in heaven and you repose in faith and hope. In this way all our misfortune and worldly care not only may be easily borne but passed off with a smile.

Prayer

I THANK thee, my heavenly Father, through Jesus Christ thy beloved Son, that thou hast preserved me this night from all danger and harm; and I beseech thee this day to safeguard me from sin and all evil, that in all my thoughts and life I may please thee. I commit my body and soul into thy hand. May thy holy angel be with me that the wicked one may have no power over me. Amen.

The Sleep of Death

4

I laid me down and slept; I awaked; for the Lord sustained me. — Psalm 3:5

THE psalmist uses words which belittle the terror of death. He says, "I lie down and sleep," rather than, "I died and was buried." For death and the grave have lost both their name and their power. Death is no longer actual death but a sleep. The grave is no longer an actual grave but a bed in which one rests. Who is not certain that he will awaken who falls into a sweet sleep where death is not present? The psalmist declares that he has not died but has slept and awakened. Just as sleep is necessary and needful to strengthen and enliven the bodily powers, so is death necessary for the betterment of life. As Psalm 4:8 suggests: "I will both lay me down in peace, and sleep: for thou, Lord, only makest me dwell in safety."

Therefore must those in Christ look not at death itself but at the certain life and resurrection, in order that the promise of John 8:51 may stand: "Verily, verily, I say unto you, If a man keep my saying, he shall never see death."

Prayer

DEAR Father, evil and pain oppress me. I suffer from unhappiness and heaviness, and I am afraid of hell. Deliver me from all of this so that thy honor, praise and will may be served. If thou dost not deliver me, may thy will not mine be done. Amen.

Giving God the Glory

5

O ye sons of men, how long will ye turn my glory into shame? how long will ye love vanity, and seek after lying? — Psalm 4:2.

To glorify God is simply to believe God, to rely upon and to love God. The man who believes God gives him the glory, certifying that he is trustworthy in all his words and promises. The man who hopes in God believes that he is mighty, wise and righteous — one from whom he can receive comfort, salvation and blessing. Such alone recognizes the power of God wherewith he can do all things, the wisdom with which he knows all things, and the goodness with which he comes to our aid.

One who does not believe in God thinks God a liar. One who does not hope in God thinks God ignorant of man's problems, unable or unwilling to help. Man will then despair of God. When man relies upon man — for the heart must believe, hope in and love something — he will trust either in riches or in friendship, his own power or some foolish fable preached by man, whether it be true or false. If he finds a crumb of comfort in it, he embraces it with his whole heart. So is the goodness of God maligned, while credit is given where it is undeserved.

Prayer

DEAR Father, may thy name be hallowed in us. I confess that I have dishonored thee, and with pride and the seeking of my personal honor and glory I blaspheme thy name. Help me, therefore, by thy grace that my name may diminish, that I may become nothing; so that thou alone and thy name and honor may be in me. Amen.

6

My voice shalt thou hear in the morning,
O Lord; in the morning will I direct my
prayer unto thee, and will look up. —
Psalm 5:3.

W HERE in the entire psalter can one read a finer prayer than this? Every consecrated Christian can learn the importance of morning meditation from the psalmist and ask that the word of God may have a firmer hold upon all who come within its hearing. "In the morning I shall pray for all the preachers and hearers of the word." Through this word God's chosen ones are fed and sustained, as Christ affirmed, "Man shall not live by bread alone, but by every word that proceedeth out of the mouth of God." When the Gospel flourishes in the church everything flourishes with it.

To direct our prayer to God we must be teachable, receptive. It calls for a mind alert, a heart prepared — the whole man joyously dedicated to his will. So let every man offer himself to God, submissive yet responsive. Let us look up that we may be enlightened and inspired, as Micah affirms: "He will bring me forth to the light, and I shall behold his righteousness." Christ gives the Holy Spirit to the Apostles and believers in order that he himself may speak in us.

Prayer

HEAVENLY Father, since no one suffers for thy sake and we are too weak to endure the killing of our old Adam nature, we beseech thee to nourish, strengthen and comfort us with thy holy word. Amen.

A Present Help for the Penitent

7

Have mercy upon me, O Lord; for I am weak: O Lord, heal me; for my bones are vexed. — *Psalm 6:2.*

THE psalmist is referring to the bones of the human body, so troubled by the spirit's weakness and fear that they tremble and cannot support the body. God often puts man into a predicament in which he no longer can depend upon human comfort and help. In this way sin is destroyed and severed from us in order that we may love God above all things and have a hearty desire for him. All earthly affections wrought in us by sin become weaker than the desire to seek God, thanks to his grace and mercy.

Perhaps I present here notions which appear unfamiliar and absurd, particularly to those who think they can find an easy way to heaven with their indulgences, their letters and their good works. I know whereof I speak.

No man will receive the mercy of God except he who fervently hungers and thirsts after him, as Psalm 42 proclaims: "As the hart panteth after the water brooks; so longs my soul, O God, for thee." Let no one imagine that a full and satisfied soul will be filled, for our God fills with good things the hungry alone.

Prayer

O FATHER, comfort and strengthen me, a poor, suffering man, with thy holy word. I cannot endure thy hand, yet I shall be condemned if I do not endure it. So strengthen me, Father, that I may not despair. Amen.

The Importance of Humility

If I have rewarded evil unto him that was at peace with me . . . let the enemy persecute my soul, and take it — *Psalm 7:4, 5.*

8

No matter how just, how holy, how true, how godly your cause may be, it is still imperative that you conduct it in fear and humility, respecting God's judgments and confiding alone in his mercy. Judas Maccabeus was defeated in a holy war, and many others have been overcome in worthy causes. Judges 1:20 describes the defeat of the children of Israel because they depended upon the rightness of their cause instead of the mercy of God.

By his own example in times of trouble David teaches us that it belongs to no one arrogantly to demand justice for himself, to justify a tumult by the rightness of his cause, and to plan revenge by power or by law. The ecclesiastics now rave and rage, hoping to appear right, clever and wise above all others. But let each stand in humble fear lest he solicit the wrath and judgment of God. He should pray for his enemies according to his conscience, since no adversary can have just cause against the man of good conscience.

Prayer

LORD GOD, thou hast placed me in thy Church. Thou knowest how unsuitable I am. Were it not for thy guidance I would long since have brought everything to destruction. I wish to give my heart and mouth to thy service. I desire to teach thy people, and long to be taught thy word. Use me as thy workman, dear Lord. Do not forsake me; for if I am alone I shall bring all to nought. Amen.

What Is Man!

9

What is man, that thou art mindful of him? and the son of man, that thou visitest him? — *Psalm 8:4.*

THE psalmist wonders at the amazing fact that a man who feels himself abandoned and forgotten by God, and is convinced above all else that God is not concerned with him, should still remain in the thought of God. It is further puzzling that a man's heart should and can retain the conviction that God is friendly, precious and good when he feels him to be angry, terrifying and unendurable. Who would not wonder at this? Who would not say: "What is man that thou art mindful of him?" This is the incomprehensible work of God, recognized through faith alone.

Who would believe that God looks on the ordinary man, since there is nothing noteworthy about him; everyone despises him. He has only this distinction that he — as all other men — was born of woman. If he were a king or prince, or a rich and powerful personality, we could more easily believe him the concern of God. But nothing more inane or despicable can be said of a person than that he is the son of man. Pilate applied that epithet to Christ: "Behold the man!" No man has much respect for another, yet God cares so much for each person that he seeks him out.

Prayer

LORD God, who hath created man and woman and ordained them for matrimony, making them fruitful by thy blessing, and hath so symbolized the union of thy beloved Son Jesus Christ and the Church; we ask thy infinite goodness that thy creation, ordinance and favor may not be disturbed or destroyed but graciously preserved; through Jesus Christ thy Son our Lord. Amen.

Blood and Tears!

10

When he maketh inquisition for blood, he remembereth them: he forgetteth not the cry of the humble. — Psalm 9:12.

WE learn here by what means the beloved apostles and martyrs have triumphed — by blood and tears. We sense, too, how far the Church of today has drifted from the Apostolic moorings. Whether this passage be applied to suffering of the past, when the first martyrs were killed by the Jews, or to the present and future persecutions under the Gentiles, makes little difference, although the text prefers the first. God remembers, in any case, the blood of the saints and does not forget the cry of the poor. Oftentimes, in fact, the conversion of persecutors takes place through the blood and tears of the martyrs. This psalm is also a warning against those who despise such friendliness and persist in their godless ways. Christ declared: "Hear what the unjust judge says, Should not God pity his elect who call to him night and day? I tell you he will avenge them speedily."

It is the duty of Christians to refrain from returning evil for evil and seeking revenge. Let us learn that each person must be patient in his cause, turning to God alone with prayers and tears. "Vengeance is mine, I will repay, saith the Lord."

Prayer

DEAR Lord God, I am thy creature—
fashioned by thee and placed here by thy
will. I have suffered grievous difficulties
and borne great trials. Give me thy grace
that I may truly recognize that I am thine
and that thou art my father. May I wait
upon thee for help and security. Amen.

Before They Call

11 Lord, thou hast heard the desire of the humble: thou wilt prepare their heart, thou wilt cause thine ear to hear.—*Psalm 10:17.*

"THOU, Lord, art so ready and willing to hear that before thy people cry unto thee, thou hast already discerned the desires of their hearts." The prophet Isaiah touches upon the same truth, "It shall come to pass, that before they call, I will answer; and while they are yet speaking, I will hear."

These words not only command us to hope when we pray but encourage us to pray when we have no such desire. These words may not stir the confident, satisfied soul but will sustain the soul that is burdened and needy. These promises are above our understanding and feeling; they must be spoken of and understood by faith alone. This psalm is a true school of faith and of the spirit. He who reads it without faith is neither warned nor enlightened. But faith lives in trials and tribulations; the sharper these are, the more brightly faith shines.

Prayer

HELP us, O God, to receive the fulfillment of all our requests. Let us not doubt that thou hast heard and will hear them; that the answer is certain not negative or doubtful. So may we say cheerfully that the outcome is true and certain. Amen.

The Look of Life

12

The Lord is in his holy temple, the Lord's throne is in heaven: his eyes behold, his eyelids try, the children of men. — *Psalm 11:4.*

DAVID specifically applies here what he has touched upon in general before. God's eyes "behold," alertly observing mankind. They not only see but examine, test, and clearly differentiate. I understand this passage as a simple allegory referring to the habit of great men of the world, who conduct their affairs with a nod of their head. Those whom they wish to favor they smile upon graciously with open eyes; those whom they hate they glower upon with narrowed eyes, a look of ferocity upon their face.

God likewise turns his eyes graciously toward the pious; but upon the godless he looks angrily. Psalm 34 bears this out: "The eyes of the Lord are upon the righteous and his ears are open unto their cry. The face of the Lord is against them that do evil, to cut off the remembrance of them from the earth." The eyelids of the Lord then are opened differently upon the righteous and the ungodly, approving the one and condemning the other.

Prayer

ALMIGHTY God, help us to suffer gladly; take away any desire for revenge. May we not repay evil with evil, or give blow for blow. May we be pleased with thy will which sends these trials, that we may so praise and thank thee. Amen.

13

"A DOUBLE heart" describes those persons who deceive others through thinking one thing and saying something else. This passage also suggests the discord of persons coming together with clashing views. Now Christ makes us to be like-minded through the pure word of God. "How good and how pleasant it is for brethren to dwell together in unity!" Acts records that "the multitude of them that believed were of one heart and of one soul," and Ephesians that "there is one faith and one Lord." Because the wicked lack the true faith, it is impossible for them to be of one heart — they must abound in party dissensions.

The Apostle Paul, therefore, admonished his readers not to be "carried about with divers and strange doctrines," for such persons were "ever learning and never able to come to the knowledge of the truth." The only likeness such people have to one another is that their words are alike without weight: each praises his own sect and labors to confirm its beliefs. Through this deceit of double-heartedness new sects are continuously being formed in our day and the unity of love is thrust aside.

Prayer

ALMIGHTY God, teach us that no man can harm us without harming himself a thousand times more in thy sight. Grant then that we may be moved more to mercy than to anger, more to pity than to resentment. Amen.

The God Who Cares

Consider and hear me, O Lord my God: lighten mine eyes, lest I sleep the sleep of death. — *Psalm 13:3.*

HOW different is the confident undertone of this psalm from those earlier ones in which David complained that he had prayed without result, that God had forgotten, turned away from and refused to listen to him. Now he is certain that his prayers will be answered. David, now victorious, prays that God may consider him, although he had been continuously heard by God. We too ask that when God thinks of us we may feel the inner joy of heart and confidence, and that we may pray for his gracious care and listen while he favors us through grace, making us victorious in life's struggle. David's prayer is not only that one may reflect upon the grace of a merciful God, but also that one may reflect upon the peace he works in men.

"Consider and hear me" means not only that God may fail to see me but also that God may fail to think of me. Come near and think of me, the psalmist pleads, that the good may be as great as the trial was before. As soon as the face of God is turned from us there follows confusion and darkness of mind, we grope about in the gloom.

Prayer

EVERLASTING and merciful God, who hath not spared thine own Son but hath given him up for us all, that he should bear our sins upon the cross, grant that our hearts may never be disturbed or discouraged in this faith. Amen.

Primacy of Faith

The fool hath said in his heart, There is
no God. — *Psalm 14:1*

THOUGH a man keep all the precepts
of God except the first, he cannot be
commended, for the first is the most important of all. Likewise is that man a
failure who lacks faith in God, however
energetic he is in living by a strict code
of right and wrong. As the first precept
is intended to be the standard, rule, and
power of the other precepts, so is faith
the head, life, and power of all good
works. No human activity is blessed unless it arises from faith, nay, unless it
is wholly anointed by faith.

But only that faith is genuine which
gives one the conviction that he has been
accepted by God, that his sins have been
forgiven and that God is gracious to him.
Of what value is faith if there is not such
a serene confidence? See how the evangelists point to our Lord's emphasis upon
faith. Jesus could perform no miracles in
the region of his nativity because of the
unbelief of its people. He warned the
disciples that they were unable to cast out
devils because of their lack of faith. Faith
alone is able to purify the heart and fulfill
all the precepts of God.

Prayer

ALMIGHTY God, dear heavenly Father, we regret that thy holy name is so often profaned, abused and dishonored in this wretched world. Many times it is not used to thy honor, and frequently it is abused by sin. So grant us thy divine grace that we may avoid all that does not augment the honor and praise of thy holy name. Amen.

On Being Neighborly

Lord, who shall abide in thy tabernacle? who shall dwell in thy holy hill? He that backbiteth not with his tongue, nor doeth evil to his neighbor, nor taketh up a reproach against his neighbor. — Psalm 15:1,3

16

ALTHOUGH two persons may be hostile to one another, the Divine Spirit does not hesitate to employ the name neighbor. By this powerful term he would move men to peace and concord, striking at their great folly. Only a madman would denounce, injure and slander his neighbor. They cannot excuse their conduct by saying that they treated their enemies just as they deserved, for that contradicts the Holy Spirit who calls them not enemies but neighbors. Against Christ, too, they sought false witnesses, they accused him, they condemned him; finally, they blasphemed him with the most vile epithets. Thus briefly but aptly has David described the life of the ungodly.

It is the duty of a good man not to take offense against his neighbor but to conceal a fault, to defend his neighbor, and where he cannot defend him, to forgive him, even though the neighbor be an adversary and an evil man. In this way the righteous man will not only refrain from harming his neighbor, but he will also do good to him in the manner of which Christ spoke: "Love your enemies, bless them that curse you, and pray for them which despitefully use you and persecute you."

Prayer

WE give thanks to thee, Lord God
Almighty, that thou hast revived us
through thy heavenly gift. We pray that
by thy mercy we may attain to a firm
faith in thee and a fervent love for one
another through Jesus Christ thy Son
our Lord. Amen.

Not by Works

17 O my soul, thou hast said unto the Lord, Thou art my Lord: my goodness extendeth not to thee. — *Psalm 16:2*

IT is very difficult to see and feel that all our goodness belongs to God and that we have nothing in ourselves by which we can merit God's applause or please him. All the theology and teaching is vain which holds that man can purchase the mercy of God by his own efforts. They fail to perceive that salvation depends upon faith and confidence in the mercy of God, and that all their own works must be lost sight of, that men must despair of them. Here can be seen the harm of that pomp of satisfaction and indulgences introduced by the heretical teachers into the Church of God. What have they taught but that we should believe God needs our good works for salvation, that our blessedness does not consist in our becoming partakers of the divine nature, and that God reaches perfection through partaking of our nature.

The title "Golden" is rightly given to this psalm, for it involves the greatest faculty — confidence in God. This faculty is the difference between the people of Christ and others. The name and fame of persons is definitely laid aside.

Prayer

OH loving God, be pleased, I pray thee, but not with the good deeds that I bring before thee. Will thou consider only this that thou art holy and friendly, and not that I am evil. Amen.

God as Refuge

Hide me under the shadow of thy wings.
— *Psalm 17:8.*

CHRIST grieves over Israel in Matthew 23:27: "How often would I have gathered thy children as a hen gathers her chickens under her wings."

The psalmist conveys the picture of a frightened child fleeing before a great danger, just as small children run for shelter to their parent's bosom and hang upon their parents neck when some fear is present. We would do well to exhibit the same atitude towards our heavenly father that he may carefully guard us when we fear the enemy. For every man deems it the greatest piety to follow the fathers and saints in their works, while few have realized that one should not duplicate their works but imitate the faith from which the works issue.

Prayer

LORD God, our heavenly Father, grant us thy help that our children may turn out well. Enable the wives and mothers to live in godly discipline and honor. May they ever remain steadfast in the love of God. Amen.

God Is Light

19

For thou wilt light my candle: the Lord my God will enlighten my darkness. — Psalm 18:28.

THAT this verse applies to the people of Christ is quite evident, for with Christ "there is no darkness at all." The teaching of these words is simply this: Proud persons have a haughty look; each one of them is his own leader, his own light. He hears no one, he believes no one, not even God himself. But Christians become ignorant that they may be wise, they despair of themselves that they may recognize his authority over them.

This light can also be likened to the word of the gospel, as Peter uses it in II Peter 1:19: "We have also a more sure word of prophecy; whereunto ye do well that ye take heed, as unto a light that shineth in a dark place, until the day dawn." In adversity and prosperity we have no other star than the word of God. Nothing is ascribed to expressions of sinful understanding or the wisdom of the flesh, which the psalmist clearly calls darkness. He pleads that this darkness may be penetrated by the light of the divine word, for the word of God alone sustains and counsels men.

Prayer

OUR Father God, I doubt not that the things for which I plead will be granted, not because I have requested them but because thou hast commanded us to pray for them and hast certainly promised them. Amen.

How I Love Thy Law!

20

More to be desired are they than gold, yea, than much fine gold: sweeter also than honey and the honeycomb. — Psalm 19:10.

THIS psalm speaks of the law of the Lord, which (through the gospel) makes itself loved. To those who desire it, it is more precious than treasure and sweeter than honey. It is undefiled, faithful, right, true, converting the soul, making wise and rejoicing the heart. This is the wonder of the Holy Spirit, who makes all things pleasing which were before displeasing. For what do men seek more zealously than riches and pleasure! Now, however, love for the law of God becomes greater than love for riches and pleasure. As soon as the Spirit comes he not only makes the law of God bearable but also enables us to long for it, so that it becomes more precious than anything we desire and more enjoyable than any pleasure.

It is evident from this passage how eminent a prophet David was, what appropriate words, figures and parables he used. He is incomparable in his ability to present profound truths in short simple words. This, then, is the fruit of evangelical preaching — the love of righteousness and the hate of all godless ways.

Prayer

ALMIGHTY God, enable us to invoke no desire but thy praise and honor when we hear something melodious or sense something pleasant. May the duplicity, falsehood and vain show of the world not seduce us. Amen.

In His Name Conquer

21 Some trust in chariots, and some in horses: but we will remember the name of the Lord our God. — *Psalm 20:7.*

CERTAINLY it takes a greater faith to venture forth in the name of the Lord than to trust in chariots and horses. Soldiers follow the second method in going into battle today; they remember previous victories to strengthen their mettle. Our Christian rulers would do well to remember the name of the Lord, from whom comes deliverance and victory. Proverbs 18:10 asserts that "the name of the Lord is a strong tower: the righteous runneth into it and is safe."

The psalmist is testifying out of his own experience. Who would suppose that a victory may be gained by the mere remembrance of the name of the Lord? But David had put it to the test. It is not enough to think upon and call upon the name of the Lord. One must persist in remembering it and think steadfastly upon it until one finally becomes victorious over all dangers which crowd him. Surely it is unthinkable that the name of the Lord should be overcome, since he is eternal and almighty; moreover, it is impossible that anyone should fail who depends upon it.

Prayer

ALMIGHTY God, through the death of thy Son thou hast destroyed sin and death, and by his resurrection hast brought innocence and eternal life, in order that we, being redeemed from the power of the devil, may abide in thy kingdom. Grant that we may believe this with a whole heart and, steadfast in faith, praise and thank thee; through thy Son Jesus Christ our Lord. Amen.

Prayer of the Heart

22 Thou hast given him his heart's desire, and hast not withheld the request of his lips. — *Psalm 21:2.*

THIS is a double description of prayer: the first part concerns the prayer of the heart, and the second the prayer of the mouth. What is the prayer of the mind except the longing of the heart; what is the prayer of the mouth except the will of the lips. Now when the lips express the words, you have the ingredients of a prayer, whereby we understand that one asks for something. The psalmist goes on to show that oral praying is not effective unless it corresponds to the desire of the heart. For what is more lively than the will and the affection. I do not know that these Davidic expressions can be found anywhere else in the scripture. The order here is beautiful, the prayer of the heart must precede, otherwise the words of the lips are without significance. The apostle Paul suggests this truth in writing to the Corinthian Christians: "I will pray with the spirit and with the understanding also."

Prayer

ALMIGHTY God, through thine infinite mercy thou not only receivest us but also commandest and teachest us, through thy beloved Son our Lord Jesus Christ, that we by his merits and means should look to thee and call thee Father. Amen.

Cry of Malediction

23

My God, my God, why hast thou forsaken me? Why art thou so far from helping me, and from the words of my roaring? — *Psalm 22:1.*

LET no one doubt that this psalm has reference to the Christ, for he uttered these words upon the cross, "My God, my God, why hast thou forsaken me?" That a special meaning belongs to this verse is evident by the evangelists' retaining them in their Aramic form in the gospels. I do not remember another place in the scriptures where the words, "My God, my God" occur. When men say that Christ's humanity was never left by his divinity, that is true. It is somewhat more puzzling to say that the human was deprived of the help of God, for who is able to make clear what this help consists of? The unlearned think that God might have delivered Christ out of the hand of the Jews, but that is not the meaning.

In Christ, there was, at the same time, the highest joy and the greatest sorrow, thorough weakness and supreme might, the purest honor and the deepest shame, the finest peace and the most vicious trouble, the fullest life and the strongest death; yet no man says "My God" who is entirely forsaken of God. Suffice it that Christ was at the same time the most righteous person and the greatest sinner, the most truly blessed and the most surely condemned.

Prayer

ALMIGHTY God, preserve us from all spiritual pride and the vainglory of temporal fame or name. Help us to call upon thy holy name in all our needs and wants. May we not forget thy holy name in the pain of conscience and in the hour of death. Grant that we in all our means, words and works may honor and praise thee alone. Amen.

The Great Shepherd

24 The Lord is my shepherd; I shall not want.
— *Psalm 23:1.*

As little as a lamb can help the shepherd in trivial things but must depend upon him for all important needs, even less can a man direct himself in the concerns of salvation or find comfort, help and guidance. Rather must he depend upon God, his shepherd, for all things, for God is infinitely more willing and active in doing all he can for his sheep than the most loving shepherd.

Christ is the gentle and tender shepherd who goes into the wilderness to seek the lost and fainting lamb, and, when he finds it, he lays it on his shoulder rejoicing. Who would not follow such a shepherd gladly! The gospel is the voice of the shepherd by which he calls his lambs. From this we learn that we receive grace, forgiveness of sins and eternal salvation. The voice of the gospel is precious to the sheep of Christ. They listen to it eagerly, understand it, and rule their lives by it. They do not heed a voice which sounds strange, but reject and flee from it.

Prayer

ALMIGHTY and Eternal God, enable us, we heartily beseech thee, to know and to praise thy dear Son as holy Simeon did, who took him in his arms, knew and confessed him; through thine own Son Jesus Christ. Amen.

Demand for Purity

25

Who shall ascend into the hill of the Lord?
or who shall stand in his holy place? He
that hath clean hands and a pure heart.
— *Psalm 24:3,4.*

A PURE heart is one that is free from
the desire and passion for evil. The psalmist does not say that a bishop, pope, doctor,
apostle, ruler or king shall stand in his
holy place. Neither does he name Greek
or Roman, the learned, wise, mighty or
rich; for with God there is no deference
paid to such titled persons. Those who
sin most grievously are not always those
who say many prayers or sing, nor those
who fast by day and maintain vigils by
night, nor those who give to the poor, nor
those who preach to the others. Finally
he refers not to those who possess high
culture and eloquence.

He alone shall stand in the holy place
who possesses these qualities: inward and
outward cleanliness, in spirit and in flesh.
Although he had all the foregoing qualities, if that were possible, it would still
profit him nothing. The Lord Jesus Christ
alone qualifies. All others are impure and
can in no way be purified by their own
abilities and efforts, but only by the grace
conferred upon them by Christ.

Prayer

GRANT us grace, our dear Father, to have before all things a vital faith in Christ, an unshakable confidence in thy mercy so that we may overcome the blindness of our erring conscience. Give us a fervent love for thee and for all men. Amen.

Sinful but Hopeful

26 For thy name's sake, O Lord, pardon mine iniquity; for it is great. — *Psalm 25:11.*

THESE words of the psalmist do not refer simply to youthful sins, but are a confession of continued transgressions even more serious than those of his past. Some people cannot understand how a Christian may be pious and righteous even while remaining a sinner. Of this the psalmist says: "I had been a sinner in my youth and yet God directed my paths. Now I am an old fool and have learned much, but still I do not do as I should." Paul, too, affirms that evil adheres to the flesh. Like that Apostle we must confess that we are evil to the extent that we rely upon an arm of flesh.

The word iniquity here stands for the deep-rooted inveterate evil. Because of it men are wicked and their sin despicable. We sometimes speak of a vice or a bad habit, but here he speaks of the primary evil which we cannot escape, only finding release from it in death. There is no counsel or doctor effective in remedying it except by living under grace. Sin is present with us, but we are not under its dominion and must not let it rule over us.

Prayer

LORD, I am thy sin, thou art my righteousness, therefore am I happy and trium-
phantly undisturbed. Thy righteousness
does not let me become nor remain a
sinner. Praise be to thee Lord and true
God to eternity. Amen.

Groping for Truth

27 For thy lovingkindness is before mine eyes: and I have walked in thy truth. — Psalm 26:3.

DAVID'S heart relies upon that loving-kindness even as he speaks: "I am on the right way for thy divine word has led me along life's journey. I have nothing before my eyes but thy goodness alone. Since my malice is also present — my heart and passions evil — I turn and hasten to thy lovingkindness." We are unable to turn ourselves, so we daily pray: "Help me, God, that my life may be lived wisely and well. I am not so spotless as to be without offense. But I have begun to walk in the way of righteousness, even though I am still rough and unsightly, and retain my sin and unrightousness."

The psalmist speaks here of the truth of God. Normally, truth is that which is right in opposition to the wrong. He is true here who is impelled by faith in God and serves his neighbor in love. True life consists simply in retaining God's word inwardly in true belief; and in outwardly living and walking according to faith.

Prayer

O FATHER, let me not fall to the doing of my own will. Break my will more and more. Whatever betides, let not my will but thine be done, for so it is in heaven. There is no self-will there. May that also be true on earth. Amen.

Serenity of Simple Trust

28

Trust in the Lord, and do good; so shalt thou dwell in the land, and verily thou shalt be fed. Delight thyself also in the Lord; and he shall give thee the desires of thine heart. — *Psalm 37:3,4.*

WITH this truth the psalmist lays aside all poignant anxieties and sets his heart at ease. Put aside your patience, my child. To curse or entertain evil thoughts is base. Set your hope upon God; wait upon his action. Render not evil for evil, but good for evil. If you desire to flee to another place, stay yet in the land where you are. Change and custom are not your dwelling place. Nourish yourself in the faith, pursue your vocation and avocation as before. Abide in the faith and entertain no doubts. God will not abandon you.

Be not annoyed that God gives prosperity to the enemy. If that is pleasing to God's will, cease your aversion to the success of the godless. He will give you the desires of your heart. What more could you wish? Exercise desire and contentment in the divine will. Then these things will not damage you, but you will be full of peace and joyfully wait for the promise of God.

Prayer

DEAR Father, may we be delivered entirely from Satan's dominion. If it please thee to leave us longer in this world of misery, grant us thy grace, that thy realm may begin and be increased in us, while the devil's dominion is retarded and destroyed. Amen.

Saviour for the Lost

29

Forsake me not, O Lord: O my God, be not far from me. Make haste to help me, O Lord my salvation. — *Psalm 38:21,22.*

WHOM did God receive but the forsaken, whom did he heal but the sick, whom did he make to see but the blind, whom did he resurrect but the dead, whom did he make holy but the sinful, whom did he instruct but the ignorant? He only comforts the miserable and gives grace to those who lack it. Thus no proud person can receive the holiness, wisdom or righteousness of God; nor can he receive the work of God, but he depends upon his own efforts, making an earthly, false, boastful saint out of himself—a hypocrite.

Hasten to help me, O God, for all others hasten to destroy! God's help is not as human help. God is not the father of the rich but of the poor—widows and orphans. He has sent the rich away empty. "O Lord my salvation" suggests that I seek no salvation or succour in myself nor in any other man but in him alone.

Prayer

TEACH us, dear Father, not to rely upon or trust in our own good deeds or means, but to venture out upon thine infinite mercy. Let us not despair because of our sinful life, but value thy mercy as higher, wider and stronger than all our life. Amen.

God, Hidden and Revealed

30

YOU must be able to think of God in two different ways: At times he is a hidden God. That condition exists when the conscience in despair feels its sins, when heart and mind are stirred, and when one is unable to be comforted by the grace and goodness of God.

There is another distinct portrayal of him as the revealed and visible—the good, gracious, merciful and redeeming God. In like manner is one sun dimmed by clouds and another shining clear and beautiful from the open heavens. First you see the sun decked with clouds and fog and giving no light; then it suddenly breaks through the clouds and fog, presenting to the world a bright and luminous appearance. So the saint comforts himself in faith, clings fast to hope, and consoles himself that God will help him to be established, so that he may go to the place of worship which God has ordained.

Prayer

WE commend to thee, heavenly Father, all who strive and work against many grievous anxieties. Strengthen those who still stand. Help raise once again those who have fallen. Amen.

Altogether Lovely

31

My heart is inditing a good matter: I speak of the things which I have made touching the king: my tongue is the pen of a ready writer. — *Psalm 45:1.*

A masterly orator, the psalmist bids his hearer listen with joy and eagerness as he relates a subject which is vital, lovely and true. Not only will he declare the truth, but he will present it in the most appealing way, in the manner of a skillful raconteur or writer.

This king is victorious, regal and strong — not with power or arms but with beauty. He does not rule by the sword but with the lips (that is, with the word). The image of Christ is revealed and proclaimed that he might attract and draw all men. This beautiful picture of Christ is the grace he reveals to us and through which he offers us all that he has done. For what can be lovelier or more attractive than Christ if man recognizes his beauty. He not only turns his face towards us but presents to us a countenance of beauty as a friendly Saviour and preserver. On this basis he rules supremely.

Prayer

ALMIGHTY God, grant that we and all Christians may receive the holy sacrament savingly by thy grace. Give us our daily bread that Christ may abide in us and we in him, and that we may worthily bear the name Christians which we have received from him. Amen.

The Presence

32

Cast me not away from thy presence; and
take not thy holy spirit from me. —
Psalm 51:11.

THE first gift the psalmist here requests
is that of the Spirit, who teaches him
how to recognize sin and to keep himself
from it. "Give me also," he pleads, "the
gift of faith that I may believe and that
sin may never again terrify me. Grant
that I, firm in the truth, may resist the
devil and his terrors, and that my confidence may not be shaken or lost." David
speaks here of a conflict which he himself
had experienced.

"Take not thy holy spirit from me," he
continues, "the Spirit which purges me of
remaining sin in order that I may live in
good conscience, discipline and honor."
There is first of all the spirit of certainty
which dissolves doubts, and affirms the
faith and also purifies both body and soul.
There is the spirit of joy, which proclaims
freedom and comfort, takes away fear and
helps one to become bolder and happier.
This gift of the Spirit works first in the
heart, then in the body and finally in one's
actions.

Prayer

O God, Father, how I am torn and tossed by this and that vice, and hindered from good works! Guard me, dear Father, and help me. Let me not yield to evil and be overcome. Amen.

What Is Man?

33

Surely men of low degree are vanity, and men of high degree are a lie; to be laid in the balance, they are altogether lighter than vanity. — *Psalm 62:9.*

THE psalmist is attempting to describe man. Man, he observes, is nothing, so one relying upon him is sure to fail. If you should put man in one balance of the scale and leave the other balance empty, the beam would tip toward the latter, thereby making man less than nothing. What the psalmist calls "vanity" here we translate as "nothing." Solomon uses this expression in Ecclesiastes: "It is vanity and vexation of spirit."

But how can man be nothing if he is the creation of God? David speaks not of the intrinsic value of the creature but of his acts. Man's faculties are good but he does not use them wisely. A ruler, king or emperor is invested with necessary powers but the citizen misuses them who relies upon and confides in them. As objects of faith they are vain and less than vanity. The psalmist does not excuse us from obeying princes; he tells us rather that we should not put confidence in them, for that belongs to God alone. The world does nothing more than to rely upon man, distrusting God. This is vain and relying upon vanity.

Prayer

HELP us, O God. How sad it is that while the light of the gospel shines, the people should be so wayward and wanton. Thou thyself shalt teach them from the word that the gospel cannot condone lives filled with avarice, gluttony, inebriation, or frivolity, resulting in greater sin and shame. Thou dost assure that those who hearken to the faith receive salvation and blessing. At such time they begin to lead a Christlike life. Amen.

Call to Prayer

34

HE who will pray and give thanks shall come to God, for there is no other like him upon the earth. But where shall one find him? Previously it was in Jerusalem but now in the Lord Jesus Christ, through whom God has presented himself to all people in all places. This is the blessing for which he is to be praised. Through this psalm we may become acquainted with him, knowing that he gladly listens to and answers our petitions.

Who is responsible when he fails to give us what we desire and need? Certainly this is no failure on his part. It is because we are too lax or lazy to pray. The psalmist is surely not deceiving us when he states that God gladly hears the prayers of all men upon earth. All flesh comes to him. If you are flesh and blood, you are hereby called and invited by this passage as much as I am, and we are invited as definitely as this or that saint. He is not alone the God of the Jews or priests but my God and the God of all who are flesh and blood. If I have been baptized in his name and believe on the same God as all others, then he will as gladly hear my prayer.

Prayer

LORD, I am not worthy that thou shouldst come under my roof, but I eagerly desire thy help and thy grace that I may be righteous. I come to thy table, having heard the gracious words of invitation. Thou dost promise me, as unworthy as I am, the forgiveness of my sins through thy body and blood if I eat and drink thereof in this sacrament. Amen.

Human Channels for Divine Truth

35 The Lord gave the word: great was the company of those that published it. — *Psalm 68:11.*

CHRIST promised his disciples a mouth of wisdom such that none of their enemies would be able to withstand them. He tells them further that they should not be concerned with what they should say, for the divine Spirit would instruct them. No sermon is of any value when God does not speak through the preacher. The apostle did not preach except when the Holy Spirit gave him utterance. Where God does not give the words, there is no sermon but vain, profitless preaching. When he speaks there are words of grace.

The word of God, however, may evoke not only peace but strife upon the earth, as Christ said: "I am not come to bring peace on earth but a sword." The weapons and warfare of the New Testament are not earthly but spiritual: not iron and arms, steed and rider but the word of God alone. As Paul says in II Corinthians 10:4, "The weapons of our warfare are not carnal, but mighty through God to the pulling down of strongholds."

Prayer

Merciful God, heavenly Father, thou
hast said to us through the mouth of thy
dear Son, our Lord Jesus Christ, "Pray
the Lord of the harvest that he will send
laborers into the harvest." Upon this thy
divine command, we pray from our hearts,
that thou wilt give thy Holy Spirit richly
to these thy servants, together with us and
all those who are called to serve thy word.
Amen.

Heart of Unbelief

36

But my people would not hearken to my voice; and Israel would none of me. So I gave them up unto their own hearts' lust: and they walked in their own counsels.
— *Psalm 81:11,12.*

ISRAEL was pleased with idols. The human heart is so constituted that it prefers lies and useless fables to the truth of God. We put our trust in a cleric's habit instead of in the God who freely promises us forgiveness of sins through his grace. We seem unable to trust God even when overwhelmed with myriads of proof from the holy scriptures. That he speaks of Israel as "my people" is even more dismaying. It would be different if a strange folk were concerned, to whom he had shown no particular deed of kindness or helped in a particular need.

Those to whom the grace and mercy of the Lord Christ is promised would not believe. They trusted in the earthly petitions of a saint, relying upon merits, fasts, watches and masses. Thus it is so difficult and dangerous to depart from the leadership of Christ, exposing oneself to all the winds of doctrine and all the deception of Satan.

Prayer

ALMIGHTY God, grant us grace to hear Jesus Christ, the heavenly bread, preached throughout the world and truly to understand him. May all evil, heretical and human doctrines be cut off, while thy word as the living bread be distributed. Amen.

God is Sovereign

37

God standeth in the congregation of the mighty; he judgeth among the gods. — Psalm 82:1.

THE psalmist clearly differentiates between the power of God and the power of the gods. God will tolerate the designation of powers over men but not over himself. God will not let them replace him but retains his ascendancy — a ruler over them all. Moses calls them gods on the ground that all authority from the highest to the lowest is ordered of God. Jehosaphat in II Chronicles said to his people: "See that you judge rightly for the judgment is of the Lord."

From this we see how highly God would have us esteem authority, that one should be obedient and submissive with fear and all honor. How foolish then for one to set himself against established authority, to be disobedient or despise rulers. God calls them after his own name and clothes them with his honor. For where there are no leaders or where they are not honored, there is no peace; where there is no peace, life is disorganized with little opportunity for teaching the word of God.

Prayer

ALMIGHTY God, grant us the forgiveness of all our sins that we, being full of grace, virtue and good works, may become thy kingdom. May we with heart, soul, mind and strength, inwardly and outwardly, submit to thy commands and do thy will. Amen.

Thine is the Kingdom

38

THE psalmist prays here for a kingdom of a superior kind, where God's name is honored, his word accepted and himself served. He speaks of the kingdom of Christ and pleads: "O God, come thyself and be judge on earth, be thyself king and Lord for the other rulers are lost. To thee belongs the kingdom among all heathen peoples in the world as promised in the scriptures."

No government is so extensive among heathen people as Christ's rule. The author does not say, "I have said you are God," but, "Arise, O God, judge the earth." Thus Christ sets in motion his divine activity. His rule embraces God's word and those who preach it. He creates and retains justice for the poor. He protects and rescues the miserable. He punishes the godless. Christianity is divine service — truth, peace, righteousness, life and salvation. Worldly justice comes to an end with this life, but the righteousness of Christ and of those in his kingdom remains unto eternity.

Prayer

ALMIGHTY God, grant us all thy grace, that we in our uncertain and miserable lives, surrounded by many foes, may fight in true faith and so receive the eternal crown. Amen.

Truth on the Scaffold

39

For the Lord will not cast off his people, neither will he forsake his inheritance. But judgment shall return unto righteousness: and all the upright in heart shall follow it. —*Psalm 94:14,15.*

THE Lord will not abandon his own people, this psalm promises. It is impossible that the godless shall carry out their designs, for if God is God they are certain to fall. "Only with thine eyes shalt thou see the reward of the wicked." If you die before you see the wicked judged, be sure you will live again and witness the justice of God meted out to them. This passage is a mighty comfort and assurance for the pious and a terrible indictment of tyrants and heretics. Its fulfillment is beyond doubt. Righteousness will bring about the right, even though — as at the present time — power passes for justice and truth. In the end both justice and hypocrisy will be overcome, but righteousness will triumph as unrighteousness is disgraced. The godly will accomplish this even though the world oppose them. Take John Hus, for example, who was condemned by the unjust power of the Roman Church. Now his righteousness has been recognized and his integrity lauded.

Prayer

ALMIGHTY God, grant that we may not be drawn by the evil and adversities of the world into impatience, revenge, anger or other vices. Help us to shun the lies, deceit and promises of the world, that we may be steadfast and daily increase in strength. Amen.

God on Our Side

40

They gather themselves together against the soul of the righteous, and condemn the innocent blood. But the Lord is my defense; and my God is the rock of my refuge. — Psalm 94:21,22.

THE unrighteous give the appearance of serenity in firm adherence to the ideas they have imagined. But when one will not accept their erroneous opinions and speaks against them, they rise up in fury and peace takes wings. The ungodly gird for conflict, they prepare all weapons, enlist authority and amass forces against us. They depend not only on the sword to enforce their doctrines but also on fire, water, earth and other elements. In shedding innocent blood they think they do God's service, but they are heretics and false teachers. Do not be discouraged; just as tyrants receive their reward so these men will not be able to avoid the judgment of God.

Our God will fulfill the promise of his word. He is on our side. No matter how the wicked strangle, imprison and persecute, I am the more certain that God is my protection. Our doctrine must prevail: their doctrine must perish. God is our defense, he will see us through whether here or elsewhere. God is our refuge, to him we flee for safety.

Prayer

I THANK thee, my heavenly Father, through Jesus Christ thy dear Son, that thou hast graciously safeguarded me this day; and I beseech thee to forgive me wherein I have erred, and preserve me this night. I commit my body and soul into thy hands. May thy holy angel be with me that the wicked one may have no power over me. Amen.

41

"I WILL behave myself wisely" — I will let God's word lead me so my course through life will be wisely directed and favorable. "In a perfect way" means in purity and blamelessly, so that I will not intermix any false faith or alloy of ideas.

This passage may well serve as a warning to governors and kings. It is a marvelous resolution which each may pursue as far as he can. David observed this in a commendable way, but most of the kings and governors did not. This kind of sincerity and activity is not the product of conscience or natural law. All rulers, when they follow nature and the highest human wisdom, must become God's enemies and persecute his word. This is as the second psalm declares: "Why do the heathen rage and the kings of the earth set themselves . . . against the Lord and against his anointed?" So poor is the record among the rulers of the Jews that scarcely three kings can be commended. With the exception of a few, including David, they ruled with the wicked, favoring the false prophets, persecuting and murdering the true prophets and condemning the word of God.

Prayer

ALMIGHTY God, let no man among us seek his own good and forget his neighbor's advantage. May we put aside all hate, envy and discord, and live with one another as the true children of God; saying in this fellowship not merely "my Father" but "our Father." Amen.

Obeying from the Heart

42

Thy people shall be willing in the day of thy power, in the beauties of holiness from the womb of the morning: thou hast the dew of thy youth. — *Psalm 110:3.*

"THE day of thy power" refers to the time of grace, when God's power shall be displayed and man's frailty shall be overcome. The scriptures speak of two periods: the first of weakness, which included those who lived under the law. At that time men did not observe the will of God freely through love but in a spirit of servile obedience. That day became to them an unbearable load and burden, impossible to enjoy. God's will must be done without compulsion and that, in the nature of the case, was impossible for them.

The second period is the covenant of grace and help through which man is made strong, willingly observes the will of God and his commands, and sincerely loves him. Christians do this not for the sake of necessity or reward, nor do they fail through suffering or death. This is not the work of nature but of grace.

Prayer

ALMIGHTY God, grant that from our good deeds and life others may be moved to praise not us but thee, and to honor thy name. Grant that no man may be led astray by our evil deeds and infirmities to dishonor thy name or neglect thy praise. May we desire nothing temporal or eternal that does not lead to the glory and the praise of thy name. Amen.

Favored of God

43 He sent redemption unto his people: he hath commanded his covenant for ever: holy and reverend is his name. — *Psalm 111:9.*

IN the crucial times of strife and war God does not forsake his own but helps them triumph over their foes. When they are imprisoned he releases them. He has fastened the tie with his people so that it cannot be undone. This bond can not be severed or voided by evil, disobedience and falsity or by the ingratitude of those who do not strive to preserve this unity. God himself will assure its preservation. This boon is surely the ground and source of all favors which he, for the sake of his bond, gives to all, having pledged that he will be their God.

Another favor is that his people will be exalted, enjoying an honorable name among the nations, as was promised them under the old covenant. Moses asserted that they should be exalted above all peoples and that God would make their name and fame extensive in the entire world.

Prayer

HEAVENLY Father, redeem us from this present sinful life. Help us to welcome the life to come and shun this evil world. May we not fear death but view it serenely. Free us from our concern for and reliance upon this present life so that thy kingdom may be fulfilled in us. Amen.

The Key to Life

44

Unto the upright there ariseth light in the darkness: he is gracious, and full of compassion and righteous. — *Psalm 112:4.*

THE light ariseth in darkness, not for the hypocrites, but for the righteous. They have riches and honor and the joy which God confers upon them. The faithful disciples will also have these blessings without sorrow. So shall they petition him, saying: "Dear Lord, give me joy and peace. It is not mine. I will not have it except it be thy will. If thou dost give it me then will I have it; but if thou dost not, so let it stand."

When one eats a sumptuous meal, or seeks pleasure without asking God for a good day, his heart shall be disconcerted so that he shall have no pleasure at all. One who keeps God before his eyes, though not eating a costly meal, shall enjoy it more thoroughly than the most wealthy. Let us therefore look to him with fear, holding him before our eyes that he may supply our needs. If we throw away our reverence for God, nothing shall be meaningful to us even though we are worth a fortune.

The righteous shall have joy and peace though they may be in darkness temporarily. The sun shall rise upon them in sorrow and trouble. God has the means by which he can give joy to those in unhappiness and comfort and peace to the sorrowful.

Prayer

FATHER, lead us not into temptation. I do not desire to be free from testings for that would be more terrible than ten temptations. But I pray that I may not fall and sin against my neighbor or thee. Amen.

Universal Yet Personal

45

Praise the Lord, all ye nations; praise him, all ye people. For his merciful kindness is great toward us: and the truth of the Lord endureth for ever. Praise ye the Lord. — *Psalm 117:1,2.*

THE psalmist proclaims with few words the great work and wonder of God — the gospel and kingdom of Christ promised at the time but still undisclosed. It is so often said that God is not alone the God of the Jew but also of the heathen, and not a small part of the heathen, but all of them scattered over the whole world. For when the author names all nations he excludes no one.

Now if all shall praise God, it must be a recognition of him as their God. As their God they must confess him, believe on him and forsake all idols, since one cannot praise God with an idolatrous mouth or with an unbelieving heart. If the nations are to believe they must first hear his word and, through it, receive the Holy Spirit. One cannot believe or receive the Spirit except he first hear the word, as Paul reminds us in Romans 10: "How shall they believe except they hear?" and in Galatians 3: "Received ye the spirit by the works of the law, or by the hearing of faith?" If the nations are to hear the word, a preacher must be sent to proclaim to them the word of God.

Prayer

ALMIGHTY God, grant that all preachers may proclaim Christ and thy word
with power and blessing everywhere. Grant
that all who hear thy word preached may
learn to know Christ and amend their
ways. Wilt thou also graciously remove
from the Church all preaching and teaching which does not honor Christ. Amen.

Secret of Serenity

46

The Lord is on my side; I will not fear:
what can man do unto me? — *Psalm 118:6.*

THE psalmist goes forward with springy steps and eternal joy testifying as to what happens when his prayers are answered. The testimony, "The Lord is on my side," is as if it were said: "My petition is heard in such a way that although the need is not yet fulfilled, I clutch a mighty support which enables me to carry my yoke softly and lightly. It is the Lord himself to whom I call, who fills my heart through his eternal word and Spirit in the midst of my need, so that I scarcely am aware of what I lack."

With such confidence, observe how alert and courageous the psalmist is, how he gambols and boasts, "I am not afraid, I am undisturbed, trials are not painful to me, I am of good courage and anxious about nothing." He defies and reproves the unbelieving world for its pride and wanton ways, declaring, "What can man do unto me!"

Prayer

W E beseech thee, O Father, to comfort our conscience now and at the hour of death. Give our hearts thy peace that we may await thy judgment with joy. Judge us not severely for then would no man be justified. Amen.

Ever Dependent upon God

47

Except the Lord build the house, they labor in vain that build it: except the Lord keep the city, the watchman waketh but in vain. — *Psalm 127:1*.

IN the first part of this passage the author condemns avarice, worry and unbelief in a family circle. In the next part he broadens his reference to an entire community. The blind world lags behind because it does not confess God and his work, but relies upon its own wisdom, understanding and power to make the community or city prosper. To that end public men amass great treasure, build strong towers, install machinery, write laws, proceeding in their own self-confidence and never once thanking God for their achievements, just as those who built the tower of Babel.

God, enthroned above, looks upon the acts of the children of men to see how cleverly and spritely they go. As Psalm 33 reminds us: "The Lord brings the counsel of the heathen to nought," and, "God knows the thoughts of man that they are vain." When one examines the history of such empires as those of the Assyrians, Babylonians, Persians, Greeks and Romans, one finds that which this verse predicts. As they rise rapidly through the wisdom of men so they are rapidly destroyed.

Prayer

ALMIGHTY God, grant that we may die willingly and peacefully, accepting it cheerfully as thy decree, that we may not in impatience or despair become disobedient to thee. May all our members — eyes, tongue, heart, head and feet — be concerned not with their own whims or will. Make them captive to thy purpose, truly controlled and subdued. Amen.

Folly of Anxiety

48

Lo, children are an heritage of the Lord:
and the fruit of the womb is his reward.
— *Psalm 127:3.*

WHERE there are no children neither house or city can exist. Now if the heir and salary are from the same God, it follows they are both God's gift, concerning which you so often worry. Why then are you troubled and anxious as to how you shall receive provisions and shelter? Though the whole world were to combine its strength, it could not duplicate the birth of a child, for this is the work of God. So why be concerned about possessions and security? If you do not have them in great abundance, why seek them? Christ makes reference to this in Matthew 6: "Is not the life more than meat, and the body than raiment?" He would explain that since something as miraculous as the birth of children is in your care, you should not be concerned with such mundane material needs as food and shelter. He who has so marvelously concealed so great a host of men in human flesh and brought them forth is the same God who gives children as an inheritance and the fruit of the body as the reward of his love. He who has given them will provide for them.

Prayer

LET us become thy heavenly children, O Father. Teach us to regard our souls highly and the heavenly inheritance alone. May our temporal and earthly possessions not deceive, ensnare or hinder us, making us children of this world. Amen.

HAVING described the fear and trial of the old nature, the psalmist now turns to the discussion of the new man as one should foster it within himself. These two ideas — fear and hope — are taught in all the psalms; indeed, in the entire scriptures. God is so good to his children that he blesses them in the midst of the disagreeable and unpleasant aspects of life. They must continue to hope, for fear is nothing else than the rise of doubt while hope is the rise of recovery. These two opposing emotions reside in us because there are two conflicting persons in us — the old and the new.

Therefore the psalmist says, "I have waited for God. From this clamor and cross I have not fled or despaired, nor have I relied upon my own ability but upon the grace of God alone. This I have desired, waited for and expected if it should please God to help me." There are some unfortunate people who want to show God the goal, and specify the time and means by which he should help them. But when it does not work out their way, they complain or seek help elsewhere. Others wait for God, pleading for grace, but leaving it to his free will as to when, how, where and by what means he will help them.

Prayer

DEAR Lord God, help me through Christ that I may never give way to blasphemy. I am aware of inward opposition to thee, but I have thy word which cannot fail me — it is my all in all. Amen.

The Open Hand of Faith

50

I stretch forth my hands unto thee: my soul thirsteth after thee, as a thirsty land. Hear me speedily, O Lord: my spirit faileth.
— *Psalm 143:6,7.*

THE wicked extend their hands but not to God. They are preoccupied with evil. But the outstretched hand of faith is a spiritual act by which we ask God to consecrate all our work. "Because my well-being depends upon thy grace," cries the psalmist, "I do nothing more than to seek thee, ever distrusting my own deeds." Thus the pious soul, in thirsting after God, accepts the truth the proud reject — all good works without God are null and void. Therefore the thoughts, words and deeds of the wicked are steeped in their own accomplishments; they are satisfied with their own lives.

How often has it been shown that the disconsolate, finding nothing in themselves, are God's loveliest offering, particularly when they implore him for grace. God hears none more fervently than he who cries and thirsts for his mercy. "I have thirsted after thy grace as long as I possibly could," cries the psalmist. "I am tired of waiting, therefore come quickly to save me." He would teach us to wait patiently for his grace, not deterred, though he seem far away and tardy to help us.

Prayer

I COME to thee and beseech thee, dear Father, to forgive me; not because I am able to earn satisfaction with my own merits but because thou hast promised and sealed it, so that it is as certain as though my forgiveness were spoken by thee. Amen.

When Tempted

51

Deliver me, O Lord, from mine enemies: I flee unto thee to hide me. Teach me to do thy will; for thou art my God: thy spirit is good; lead me into the land of uprightness. — *Psalm 143:9,10.*

THE psalmist complains, "My foes do not trust thee nor thy rule, and so they do not flee to thee. They presume to instruct me as to what I should do and would be masters over all. Protect me from them," he pleads, "and be thyself my Master." Compare this passage with Psalm 119, "O God, redeem my soul from lying lips" — that is, false doctrine and cunning lips which teach error in the guise of truth.

"Thou art my God." "I do not make an idol out of my wisdom and righteousness," says the psalmist, "as my enemies do. But I rely upon thy grace and partake of the wisdom and righteousness which is in thee now and ever. Do not permit the wicked to lead me or any man, for they follow crooked paths, led by the evil spirit." The good spirit is the Holy Spirit who fashions meek, gentle, and good hearts which follow the right way, seeking not themselves but God in all things.

Prayer

THY will be done, dear Father, and not the will of the devil or our enemies, nor those who would persecute and destroy thy holy word or hinder the coming of thy kingdom. Enable us all patiently to suffer what we have to bear and conquer, so that our poor flesh may not waver or fail through weakness or indolence. Amen

Smile of Peace

He maketh peace in thy borders, and filleth thee with the finest of the wheat. — Psalm 147:14.

52

PEACE is another of God's favors. Not only is there blessing and progress in the city, but the land is ringed about with peace and prosperity so that man can walk, plough, and plant. This calls to mind pious, loyal neighbors, obedient princes and peasants. There is an expression that no man can have peace longer than his neighbor wants him to, and to have an evil neighbor is surely not the least of misfortunes. Neighborliness is more conducive to peace than unlimited quantities of weapons and the protection of iron battlements. The ancients agreed, as Terentius, for example, who said: "He who thinks that a state is more stable which must be held by power than abides by friendship of the people, I hold to be in grievous error." Aristotle, too, affirmed that what is held together by power does not have the truth. Solomon expressed his preference in Proverbs 27: "Better is a neighbor that is near than a brother far off." What good is it if one has a thousand brothers, all of whom live far from him? I would prefer a good neighbor above all.

Prayer

ALMIGHTY God, thou desirest us not only to call thee Father but our Father, that we may pray unitedly for all people. Give us fraternal affection that we may recognize each other as true brothers and sisters, and petition thee as our common Father for all mankind as one child pleads with its father for another. Amen.